Jump Start Your Career
in Technology & IT
in about 100 Pages

Table of Contents

Let's Start !

Introduction

This book will introduce you to the world of globalization and localization. The goal is to give you a deeper understanding of how to write applications that support different languages and cultures. I'll guide you through the basics and then go into different implementations.

The book is primarily focused on .NET.

The book also contains strategies for web development. The examples for web development are written using ASP.NET MVC and JavaScript/Globalize. You can however apply the sample principles in any other type of application.

In the book I'll be using .NET 4. There are some minor changes compared to earlier versions. You can for instance assign a neutral culture to `CurrentCulture` (see first chapter for more information). There are also some new features in .NET 4.5 that have not been included in this book.

Throughout this book I'll skip the terms localization (i10n), internationalization (i18n) and globalization. If you look them up, you'll find as many definitions as there are developers.

Let's just say that we've written applications that work well for you and me.

 Note: All examples can be downloaded from https://github.com/jgauffin/books/tree/master/Localization.

Chapter 1 Starting with localization

Every spoken language has its own rules of formatting when it comes to dates, currency, and numbers. Rules vary from how a date is printed to what the thousand separator is for numbers. These rules can also vary for the same language, but from country to country.

Localization is about formatting all information that we present in a way that is familiar to the user. Thankfully for us, most of these rules have already been captured and implemented in .NET and the JavaScript plugin Globalize.

All code examples that do not include a method must be placed in one, for instance in a new Console project. You must also add a using to `System.Globalization`.

Cultures

To be able to control how to format information we must have some ways to represent the language and country that we are targeting. In most programming languages, this identification is made through a string called culture code.

The culture code itself consists of two parts delimited by an underscore or a colon. The actual delimiter varies between programming languages. A string can be "sv-FI" representing Swedish language as spoken in Finland or "en-US" for English as spoken in the US.

The first part of the code is one of the codes defined in ISO639, and the country code is defined in ISO3166. The actual combination is defined in RFC4646, which is a 59-page long document.

Neutral Culture

The neutral culture is used to format strings in a generic way for a language, meaning it doesn't adopt the formatting for a specific country, but for the language in general.

Neutral cultures are identified by strings where the country is omitted. For example, "en" instead of "en-US".

Invariant culture

I prefer to see the invariant culture as the coding culture. It formats strings and numbers just as we write them in our code. For instance, with no digit grouping and a dot as the decimal separator.

Hence it's also a great format to use if you have to store information as strings, as the culture will never change.

.NET

Most of the language/culture handling in .NET is controlled by a single class called **CultureInfo**. It defines the language to use and how things like numbers and dates should be formatted. All classes used for localization are provided in that namespace.

.NET contains a set of built-in combinations that you can use without any additional configuration. These are defined in the following MSDN article. The linked article does not include Windows 8, but all codes work in Windows 8 too. You can also generate your own cultures using the **CultureAndRegionInfoBuilder**.

Two different cultures exist in .NET. The first one is called UICulture and controls which language the user interface should be presented in. The other one is just called Culture, which controls formatting of strings and numbers. They are both set through the current thread using the **Thread.CurrentThread.CurrentCulture** and **Thread.CurrentThread.CurrentUICulture** classes.

User interface culture

This culture is by default set to reflect the installed OS language, i.e., the language that all strings are in (for instance in the Start menu in Windows as shown in the following figure).

Figure 1: OS Language

The "formatting" culture

There is another culture setting which represents formats used for dates, strings, currency etc. Unless you have specified a value, by default it's the same setting in Windows, as shown in the following figure.

Figure 2: Changing regional formatting

You can assign a new culture like this:

```
static void Main(string[] args)
{
    Thread.CurrentThread.CurrentCulture = new CultureInfo("sv-SE");
    Thread.CurrentThread.CurrentCulture = new CultureInfo(1053); //Swedish
locale name
}
```

There are two shortcuts that can be used to access the culture settings. They provide read-only access to the culture settings.

```
static void Main(string[] args)
{
    Thread.CurrentThread.CurrentCulture = new CultureInfo("sv-SE");
    Console.WriteLine(CultureInfo.CurrentCulture.Name); // Prints "sv-SE"
}
```

Operating system culture

You can also access the culture that the operating system was installed with. The property is named **CultureInfo.InstalledUICulture**.

Formatting using the invariant culture

To format using the invariant culture simply pass it to the **ToString()** method:

```
static void Main(string[] args)
{
    var number = 22.30;
    var result = number.ToString(CultureInfo.InvariantCulture);
    Console.WriteLine(result); // Prints "22.30"
    Console.ReadLine();
}
```

RegionInfo

.NET also contains a class called **RegionInfo** that provides information about a country. For instance, you can use it to get the current currency symbol or to determine if the metric system is used:

```
static void Main(string[] args)
{
    var info = new RegionInfo("sv-SE");
    Console.WriteLine("Uses the metric system: {0}", info.IsMetric);
    Console.WriteLine("I wish I had 100 {0}", info.CurrencySymbol);
}
```

Figure 3: Result form code example

JavaScript

JavaScript has support for basic formatting and parsing. But it is just that: basic. For example, you cannot control if a short or long format should be used or how many decimals to include.

I'm therefore going to use the Globalize plugin in all code examples where vanilla JavaScript is not enough.

Discovering the culture

You can use the client side to specify which culture to use. It's typically done with the help of the "*Accept-Language*" header. It contains the languages that the user understands, in the order in which order he/she prefers them. The following figure shows an example of the header.

▼ **Request Headers**   view source
　　Accept: text/html,application/xhtml+xml,application/xml;q=0.9,*/*;q=0.8
　　Accept-Charset: ISO-8859-1,utf-8;q=0.7,*;q=0.3
　　Accept-Encoding: gzip,deflate,sdch
　　Accept-Language: en-US,en;q=0.8,sv;q=0.6

Figure 4: Accept-Language header

The setting itself is specified through your web browser settings. Since Internet Explorer is configured using the regional settings in Windows, I've included an sample for Google Chrome. You can find the setting for Google Chrome under "Advanced" as demonstrated by the following figure:

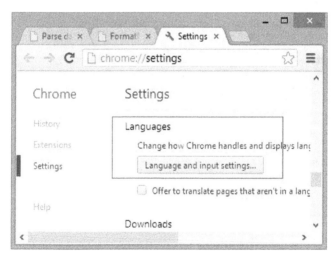

Figure 5: Chrome regional settings

To access that setting you can use **window.navigator.language** in JavaScript. That property does not exist in IE, however. Instead you have to combine it with the IE property like this:

```
var language = window.navigator.userLanguage || window.navigator.language;
```

Do note that the IE property does not return the browser language, but the specified language in IE or the Windows Control Panel (it depends on the IE version).

The JavaScript methods

JavaScript has a couple of functions that you can use to localize strings, such as **toLocaleString** and **toLocaleDateString**. However, the support is different depending on the browser. You can only expect the browser to format using the culture that the browser was installed with (or at worst using the OS culture).

Note that some of the methods do allow you to specify the culture as an argument, and the support will be probably improved over time.

Hence I'm going to show you JS examples that use those methods, but also using the alternative below.

Globalize

Globalize is a JavaScript plugin that has excellent support for different cultures and various formatting formats.

It's an open source library maintained by the jQuery foundation. The library itself is standalone, however, and not dependent of jQuery.

To use Globalize, we have to include the script itself in the HTML header:

```
<script src="http://ajax.aspnetcdn.com/ajax/globalize/0.1.1
/globalize.min.js"></script>
```

However, that script only contains all the handling. We also have to include the cultures that define all rules for each specific country/language. We can either include only the cultures that we need, or use the script that includes all cultures:

```
<script src="http://ajax.aspnetcdn.com/ajax/globalize/0.1.1/cultures
/globalize.cultures.js"></script>
```

To switch culture using Globalize we can either change by globally setting the culture:

```
Globalize.culture("se-SE");
```

But we can also specify the culture in every method that we invoke:

```
<script type="text/javascript">
    // Says that we want to parse the string as Swedish
    var result = Globalize.parseFloat("1234,56", 10, "sv-SE");

    // output using the default culture (i.e. en-US)
    document.writeln(Globalize.format(result, "n2"));
</script>
```

The result is shown in the following figure.

Figure 6: Number output

Globalize is available at github.

Summary

The goal of this chapter is to introduce you to the settings that control how the language and formatting is made in .NET.

The effects of these settings will be discussed throughout this book.

You can read more about **CultureInfo** in MSDN.

Chapter 2 Date and time

Date and time settings might be seem to be trivial, but they actually vary a lot. Without a proper library parsing date,time strings would be confusing.

The string "*1/2/2003*" can actually be interpreted both as second of January and first of February depending on which country you live in. Here in Sweden we do not use that format at all, but instead "*2003-02-01*" (yes, the zeroes should be included).

As for the time, it typically only differs in whether a 12-hour or 24-hour format should be used.

The standard format

There is an ISO standard that specifies how date and time should be formatted. The standard is called ISO8601. The common denominator is that the order should be from the most significant to least significant.

Dates should be formatted as:

YYYY-MM-DD => 2013-05-13

Time should be formatted as:

HH:MM:SS => 23:00:10

And finally the combination:

YYYY-MM-DDTHH:MM:SS => 2013-05-13T23:00:10

String representation

Sometimes you have to represent a date as a string, typically when you exchange information with other systems through some sort of API, or use UI binding.

Using just date/time strings like "2013-01-01 01:39:20" is ambiguous since there is no way of telling what time zone the date is for. You therefore have to use a format that removes the ambiguity.

I recommend you use one of the following two formats.

RFC1123

The first format is the one from RFC1123 and is used by HTTP and other Internet protocols. It looks like this:

Mon, 13 May 2013 20:46:37 GMT

HTTP requires you to always use GMT as time zone while the original specification allows you to use any of the time zones specified in RFC822. I usually follow HTTP, as it makes the handling easier (i.e. use UTC everywhere except in the user interaction; more about that later).

RFC3339

RFC3399 is based upon several standards like ISO8601. Its purpose is to make the date rules less ambiguous. It even includes ABNF grammar that explains the format that ISO8601 uses.

To make it simple: use the letter "T" between the date and time, and end the string with the time zone offset from UTC. UTC itself is indicated by using Z as a suffix.

UTC time:

2013-05-13T20:46:37Z

Central European time (CET)

2013-05-13T20:46:37+01:00

.NET

The date/time formatting is controlled by the **CultureInfo.CurrentCulture** property. Try to avoid using your own formatting (i.e. manually specify the format), as it rarely works with different cultures. Instead just make sure that the correct culture has been specified and use the formatting methods which are demonstrated below.

```
var currentTime = DateTime.Now;
Console.WriteLine("Full formats");
Console.WriteLine(currentTime.ToString());
Console.WriteLine(currentTime.ToString("R"));
Console.WriteLine();
Console.WriteLine("Time");
Console.WriteLine(currentTime.ToShortTimeString());
Console.WriteLine(currentTime.ToLongTimeString());

Console.WriteLine();
Console.WriteLine("Date");
Console.WriteLine(currentTime.ToShortDateString());
Console.WriteLine(currentTime.ToLongDateString());
```

```
Console.WriteLine();
```

The result is shown in the following figure.

```
file:///C:/Users/jgauffin/Dropbox/Books/Locali...  -  □  ×

Full formats
2013-02-28 19:22:34
Thu, 28 Feb 2013 19:22:34 GMT

Time
19:22
19:22:34

Date
2013-02-28
den 28 februari 2013

Press enter
```

Figure 7: Standard ToString() formats

RFC1123

There are some formatters for **DateTime.ToString()** that can be used, such as "R," which will return an RFC1123 time as mentioned in the previous section.

```
Console.WriteLine(DateTime.UtcNow.ToString("R"));
```

The output is:

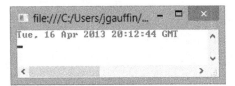

```
file:///C:/Users/jgauffin/...  -  □  ×

Tue, 16 Apr 2013 20:12:44 GMT
```

Figure 8: UtcNow as RFC1123

Do note that "R" defines that the date is GMT no matter what time zone you are in. It's therefore very important that you use **UtcNow**, as in the example above. I'll come back to what UTC/GMT means in the next chapter.

RFC3339

As the **DateTime** structure in C# does not have time zone information, it's impossible for it to generate a proper RFC3339 string.

The code below uses an extension method, which is defined in the appendix of this book.

```
var cetTime = DateTime.Now.ToRFC3339("W. Europe Standard Time");
```

The code generates the following string (Daylight saving time is active):

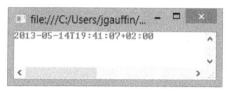

Figure 9: RFC3339

Time zones are discussed in more detail in a later chapter.

Formatting by culture

You can also format dates by specifying cultures explicitly.

```
var currentTime = DateTime.Now;

var swedish = new CultureInfo("sv-se");
Console.WriteLine("Swedish: {0}", currentTime.ToString(swedish));

var us = new CultureInfo("en-us");
Console.WriteLine("US: {0}", currentTime.ToString(us));

var china = new CultureInfo("zh-CN");

Console.WriteLine("China: {0}", currentTime.ToString(china));
```

The result follows:

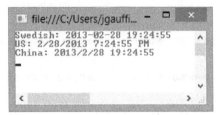

Figure 10: Time in different cultures

If you are interested in seeing how each culture formats its dates, go to the Control Panel and open up the **Region** applet as the following figure demonstrates:

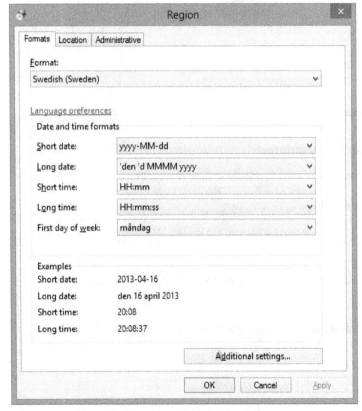

Figure 11: Control Panel for regional settings

Simply select a new culture to see its formats.

Figure 12: Date Format

Parsing dates

Parsing dates can be a challenge, especially if you do not know in advance the culture on the user's system, or if it is different from the one in the application server (for instance in web applications).

Here is a simple example that shows how the exact same string can be interpreted differently.

```
class Program
{
    static void Main(string[] args)
    {
        var date = DateTime.Parse("1/2/2003", new CultureInfo("sv"));
        var date2 = DateTime.Parse("1/2/2003", new CultureInfo("fr"));
        Console.WriteLine(date.ToLongDateString() + " vs " +
date2.ToLongDateString());
    }
}
```

The sample output is:

Figure 13: Different date formats for cultures

The parser is quite forgiving, as "1/2/2003" is not a valid date string in Sweden. The real format is "YYYY-MM-DD". This also illustrates another problem: If anyone had asked me to mentally parse "1/2/2003," I would have said the first of February and nothing else.

A forgiving parser can be a curse as it can interpret values incorrectly. As in such, you may think that you have a correct date when you don't.

You can force exact parsing if you know the kind of format (as in long or short format):

```
class Program
{
    static void Main(string[] args)
    {
        var swedishCulture = new CultureInfo("sv-se");

        // incorrect
        var date = DateTime.Parse("1/2/2003", swedishCulture);
        Console.WriteLine(date);

        // throws an exception
        try
        {
            var date2 = DateTime.ParseExact("1/2/2003",
                swedishCulture.DateTimeFormat.ShortDatePattern,
                swedishCulture);
        }
        catch (Exception ex)
        {
            Console.WriteLine(ex.Message);
        }


        // OK.
        var date3 = DateTime.ParseExact("2003-02-01",
            swedishCulture.DateTimeFormat.ShortDatePattern,
            swedishCulture);
        Console.WriteLine(date3);

        Console.ReadLine();
    }
}
```

The output follows:

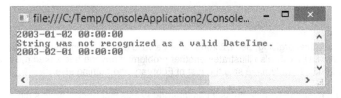

Figure 14: Date parsing.

Notice that the format is retrieved from .NET and is nothing that I supply through a string constant. It's a nice way to get around the forgiving parser to be sure that the parsed value is correct.

JavaScript

We use the Globalize plugin to handle date/time in HTML pages.

```html
<html>
<head>
    <title>Parse date example</title>
    <script src="http://ajax.aspnetcdn.com/ajax/jquery/jquery-
1.9.0.min.js"></script>
    <script
src="http://ajax.aspnetcdn.com/ajax/globalize/0.1.1/globalize.min.js"></scrip
t>
    <script
src="http://ajax.aspnetcdn.com/ajax/globalize/0.1.1/cultures/globalize.cultur
es.js"></script>
</head>
<body>
    <script type="text/javascript">

        Globalize.culture("en");
        var enResult = Globalize.parseDate("1/2/2003", null, "fr");
        Globalize.culture("fr");
        var frResult = Globalize.parseDate("1/2/2003");

        document.writeln("EN: " + enResult + "<br>");
        document.writeln("FR: " + frResult + "<br>");

    </script>
</body>
</html>
```

The result is:

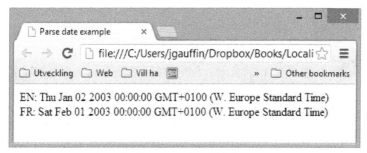

Figure 15: Date output from Globalize

You can also pass the culture as a parameter:

```
<script type="text/javascript">
    var enResult = Globalize.parseDate("1/2/2003", null, "en");
    var frResult = Globalize.parseDate("1/2/2003", null, "fr");

    document.writeln("EN: " + enResult + "<br>");
    document.writeln("FR: " + frResult + "<br>");
</script>
```

Chapter 3 Week numbers

Week numbers are complicated, since there are different ways to calculate which week it is. The ISO week always starts on Monday. The first week of the year is either calculated by finding the first of January or the week including January 4th.

The first week of 2013 started with 31st of December this year, while it started with the 2nd of January the year before. But that's if you follow the ISO specification as shown in the Swedish calendar below.

Calendar for January 2012 (Sweden)

			January				
Week	Mon	Tue	Wed	Thu	Fri	Sat	Sun
52							1
1	2	3	4	5	6	7	8

Figure 16: Swedish calendar

In the United States, (amongst several countries) the week starts with Sunday, and the first week of the year begins with January 1st.

Calendar for January 2012 (United States)

			January			
Sun	Mon	Tue	Wed	Thu	Fri	Sat
1	2	3	4	5	6	7

Figure 17: US calendar

.NET

To get the week of the year you simply invoke:

```
using System.Globalization;
using System.Threading;

class Program
{
    static void Main(string[] args)
    {
        var theDate = new DateTime(2012, 1, 1);

        Thread.CurrentThread.CurrentCulture = new CultureInfo("sv-SE");
        var calendar = CultureInfo.CurrentCulture.Calendar;
        var formatRules = CultureInfo.CurrentCulture.DateTimeFormat;
        var week = calendar.GetWeekOfYear(theDate,
formatRules.CalendarWeekRule, formatRules.FirstDayOfWeek);
        Console.WriteLine("SE week: " + week);


        Thread.CurrentThread.CurrentCulture = new CultureInfo("en-US");
        calendar = CultureInfo.CurrentCulture.Calendar;
        formatRules = CultureInfo.CurrentCulture.DateTimeFormat;
        week = calendar.GetWeekOfYear(theDate, formatRules.CalendarWeekRule,
formatRules.FirstDayOfWeek);
        Console.WriteLine("US week: " + week);

        Console.ReadLine();
    }
}
```

The output follows:

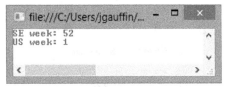

Figure 18: Different week numbers for first week of year.

The first week of year bug

However, if we examine the calendar in Windows it will show the following for January 2013:

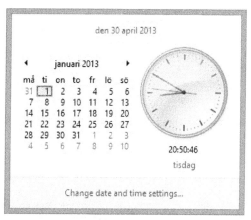

Figure 19: Week bug

By the ISO definition, the 31st of December should be part of week 1, 2013. Let's prove that with some code:

```
using System.Globalization;
using System.Threading;

class Program
{
    static void Main(string[] args)
    {
        var theDate = new DateTime(2013, 12, 31);

        var calendar = CultureInfo.CurrentCulture.Calendar;
        var week = calendar.GetWeekOfYear(theDate,
CalendarWeekRule.FirstFourDayWeek, DayOfWeek.Monday);
        Console.WriteLine("ISO week: " + week);


        Console.ReadLine();

    }
}
```

The result follows:

Figure 20: ISO week number

That's the only exception that I've found. If you try January the 6th it will show week 1, and January the 7th will show week 2.

JavaScript

Neither JavaScript nor Globalize has a method for getting the week number. There are several scripts out there which can do that. Here is one that I found at stackoverflow.com.

```
/* For a given date, get the ISO week number
 *
 * Based on information at:
 *
 *    http://www.merlyn.demon.co.uk/weekcalc.htm#WNR
 *
 * Algorithm is to find nearest thursday, it's year
 * is the year of the week number. Then get weeks
 * between that date and the first day of that year.
 *
 * Note that dates in one year can be weeks of previous
 * or next year, overlap is up to 3 days.
 *
 * e.g. 2014/12/29 is Monday in week  1 of 2015
 *      2012/1/1   is Sunday in week 52 of 2011
 */
function getWeekNumber(d) {
    // Copy date so don't modify original
    d = new Date(d);
    d.setHours(0, 0, 0);
    // Set to nearest Thursday: current date + 4 - current day number
    // Make Sunday's day number 7
    d.setDate(d.getDate() + 4 - (d.getDay() || 7));
    // Get first day of year
    var yearStart = new Date(d.getFullYear(), 0, 1);
    // Calculate full weeks to nearest Thursday
    var weekNo = Math.ceil((((d - yearStart) / 86400000) + 1) / 7)
    // Return array of year and week number
    return [d.getFullYear(), weekNo];
```

```
}
```

You can use it like this:

```
var d = new Date();
document.writeln(getWeekNumber(d));
```

However, I prefer to extend the date object with the method instead.

```
Date.prototype.getWeekNumber =  function()
{
// the code here
}
```

Which allows us to:

```
document.writeln(d.getWeek());
```

Chapter 4 Time zones

Time is not the same all over the world. When I go home from work (in Sweden), citizens in New York are having lunch.

The tricky part is handling different time zones within in the same application.

Universal Coordinated Time

UTC is ground zero. It's the time zone on which all other time zones are based. It is also known as GMT (Greenwich Mean Time). The purists do however discourage you from using the GMT name, as it's not as exact as UTC. It doesn't have a definition of leap seconds to compensate for the earths slowing rotation.

Different time zones are illustrated below:

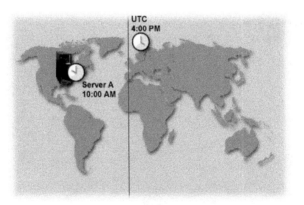

Figure 21: Time zones (Image courtesy of IBM.)

UTC does not have support for Daylight Saving Time (DST). In fact, the majority of countries do not observe DST. The image below illustrates that.

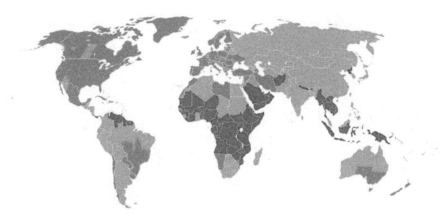

Image courtesy of _Wikipedia_

▌ DST observed
▌ DST formerly observed
▌ DST never observed

Figure 22: DST usage

Handling different time zones

It can get complicated if you want to display dates for users in different time zones but store the date entered by the user (or by the client application). Have you ever visited an online forum where you wonder what the date/time really represents? See below for an illustration.

Figure 23: Time zone confusion

The answer to the question is that 12:00 means that the US user posted the message one hour ago.

A good practice is therefore to always use UTC (Universal Coordinated time) internally in your applications. It simplifies processing since you never have to think about which time zone you are currently representing. It also removes any need to do conversions other than between two different user time zones.

You should only use local time in the user interactions, like when displaying dates or letting the user specify dates in your forms.

The image below illustrates what I mean.

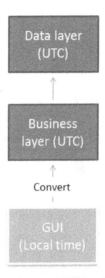

Figure 24: Usage of local time and UTC time in applications

The great thing with this approach is that the user will always see time and date using their own time zone, no matter which user saved the entry.

Client/server guideline

With client/server I mean all forms of communication where you either send or receive information from another process, like with a REST (REpresentational State Transfer) API or a messaging system like MSMQ (Microsoft Messaging Queues).

I recommend you use UTC anytime you either consume or produce information for your clients. You might know where your client applications are located, but do you know where the client application users are?

It's therefore better to expose UTC and let the client decide whether or not to do a time zone conversion.

Also, make it clear that you expect to get UTC in all requests sent by the client.

.NET

The **DateTime** structure does not specify what time zone it is for. It just contains a date/time. That's actually a really good decision, since anything else could lead to a mess. What kind of result would you expect from performing an addition between two date/times in different time zones?

Notice that the .NET Framework offers a date/time structure, which has support for time zones (**DateTimeOffset**). Use it in applications that require it, like those developed for Windows 8, WinRT, and Windows Phone.

In other cases it can make sense to avoid it since most developers are more used to **DateTime**. In those cases it might be more straightforward to use UTC internally as described earlier.

Listing time zones

All available time zones can be listed by using the **System.TimeZoneInfo** class. It will return all time zones available.

```
class Program
{
    static void Main(string[] args)
    {
        foreach (var timeZone in TimeZoneInfo.GetSystemTimeZones())
        {
            Console.WriteLine(timeZone.DisplayName);

        }
    }
}
```

The result follows:

```
file:///C:/Users/jgauffin/Dropbox/Books/Localization/Example/DataTime/List tim...   –  □  ×
(UTC+08:00) Krasnoyarsk
(UTC+08:00) Kuala Lumpur, Singapore
(UTC+08:00) Perth
(UTC+08:00) Taipei
(UTC+08:00) Ulaanbaatar
(UTC+09:00) Irkutsk
(UTC+09:00) Osaka, Sapporo, Tokyo
(UTC+09:00) Seoul
(UTC+09:30) Adelaide
(UTC+09:30) Darwin
(UTC+10:00) Brisbane
(UTC+10:00) Canberra, Melbourne, Sydney
(UTC+10:00) Guam, Port Moresby
(UTC+10:00) Hobart
(UTC+10:00) Yakutsk
(UTC+11:00) Solomon Is., New Caledonia
(UTC+11:00) Vladivostok
(UTC+12:00) Auckland, Wellington
(UTC+12:00) Coordinated Universal Time+12
(UTC+12:00) Fiji
(UTC+12:00) Magadan
(UTC+12:00) Petropavlovsk-Kamchatsky - Old
(UTC+13:00) Nuku'alofa
(UTC+13:00) Samoa
```

Figure 25: Time zone list result

The **System.TimeZoneInfo** class can be used to do the following:

- Retrieve all previously defined time zones: TimeZoneInfo.GetSystemTimeZones()
- Convert date/time between two time zones: TimeZoneInfo.ConvertTime()
- Create a new time zone (if missing amongst the predefined ones).

Conversion in fat clients

If you are running desktop applications (such as WPF) on fat clients, you can get the current time zone (i.e. the time zone configured in the operating system for the current user) like this:

```
class Program
{
    static void Main(string[] args)
    {
        var zone = TimeZone.CurrentTimeZone;
        Console.WriteLine("I'm in timezone '{0}'", zone.StandardName);
        Console.WriteLine("Daylight saving time is on? {0}",

        zone.IsDaylightSavingTime(DateTime.Now));
    }
}
```

The result follows:

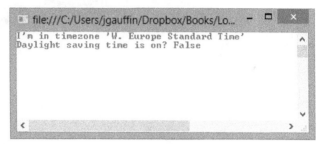

Figure 26: Result from DST check

And you can do conversions like this:

```
class Program
{
    static void Main(string[] args)
    {
        var currentTime = DateTime.Now;
        Console.WriteLine("Local time: '{0}'", currentTime);

        var universal = currentTime.ToUniversalTime();
        Console.WriteLine("Universal time '{0}'", universal);

        var localAgain = universal.ToLocalTime();

    Console.WriteLine("Local time '{0}'", localAgain);
    }
}
```

The result is:

Figure 27: UTC to local time conversion

Conversions in client/server

The client isn't always a .NET application that can provide UTC times to you. However, the client needs to provide the time zone in some way by either using the name, like "W. Europe Standard Time" or by using the base offset (without Daylight Saving Time) like "01:00."

If you got that information, you can do something like this (using the extension methods in the Appendix):

```
class Program
{
    static void Main(string[] args)
    {
        // local time specified by the user
        var dt = new DateTime(2013, 5, 14, 19, 46, 00);

        // if the user is in central Europe
        var cet = dt.ToUniversalTime(TimeSpan.FromHours(1));
        var cet2 = dt.ToUniversalTime("W. Europe Standard Time");

        // if the user is in PST
        var pst = dt.ToUniversalTime(TimeSpan.FromHours(-8));
        var pst2 = dt.ToUniversalTime("Pacific Standard Time");

        // the standard .NET way
        var cet3 = new DateTimeOffset(dt,
TimeSpan.FromHours(1)).ToUniversalTime();

    var pst3 = new DateTimeOffset(dt, TimeSpan.FromHours(-8)).ToUniversalTime();

    }
}
```

JavaScript

Web applications are like client/server applications, except that you have no control over the client. We have the same problems, but we have no control over what the client sends to us by default.

Since web applications are client/server-based, we are depending of one of the following options: That the client supplies us with the user time zone, or the client automatically converts date and time to/from UTC.

The problem is that HTTP does not have a standard header that could supply us with the user time zone. That basically means that it's up to us to figure out a way to handle the time zone.

It's not possible to use HTML only to handle the time zone. Instead we have to use JavaScript. Getting the time zone is quite easy. We can use the Date object for that, create a new HTML page and paste the following:

```
<html>
<body>
<script type="text/javascript">

    document.write(new Date().getTimezoneOffset());

</script>
</body>

</html>
```

We get the following result:

Figure 28: Javascript output for timezone offset

The above example will print **-60** for the Swedish time zone (UTC+1) since we have to subtract 60 minutes to get a UTC time. Powered with that knowledge, let's do a simple conversion from local time to UTC:

```
<html>
<body>
<script type="text/javascript">

    var localTime = new Date();
    var utc = new Date(localTime.getTime() +
localTime.getTimezoneOffset()*60000);
    document.writeln(localTime + "<br>");
    document.writeln(utc + "<br>");

</script>
</body>
</html>
```

The result is:

Figure 29: Attempt to change time zone

The time is right, but the time zone is wrong. We didn't supply a time zone, so JavaScript just thought that we wanted to display a specific time in the current time zone.

Let's examine that a bit by creating a date/time where we explicitly specify the time zone:

```html
<html>
<body>
<script type="text/javascript">

        var utc = new Date("Thu Feb 28 2013 19:38:41 GMT+0");
        document.writeln(utc + "<br>");

</script>
</body>
</html>
```

The result follows:

Figure 30: Parsing date string

The thing is that JavaScript will always implicitly convert all specified times to the user time zone. Hence it can get confusing quickly if we do not handle UTC in some other way.

Let's do a small elaboration. The number **1356350400000** represents the number of seconds from January 1, 1970 to 12:00 on December 24, 2012. Those kind of numbers are called UNIX times. What happens if we create a JavaScript **Date()** object from it?

```html
<html>
<body>
<script type="text/javascript">

        var time = new Date(1356350400000);
        document.writeln(time + "<br>");

</script>
</body>

</html>
```

The result is:

Figure 31: Parsing UNIX time

That means that any supplied UNIX time should be in UTC format. Hence we can use UNIX times to represent UTC and **Date** objects to represent local time.

We could now use two different strategies to deal with time zones. We either handle everything at client side (in the browser) or transport the time zone to the server and let the server deal with the conversion.

Sending the time zone to the server

Sending the time zone is easy to do if cookies are enabled. Simply create a session cookie (i.e. a cookie which expires when the browser window is closed) that contains the time zone. You can create a session cookie in ASP.NET by using **Response.SetCookie** with a new cookie that has not specified an expiration time.

Well, it could be that simple. But the fact is that not everyone allows cookies. Hence we must consider that cookies could be turned off. The best approach to take is to have a minimal front page which just directs to the real page (with the cookie set).

By doing so we can gracefully downgrade to just use the default time zone (if no cookies were sent to the second page).

Note: Since .NET doesn't have much of a concept of user time zones in the scope of client/server applications, you can never use DateTime.ToUniversalTime() to convert from the time specified by the user to UTC. That method will only convert from the client time zone (the time zone for the web server) to UTC.

The entry page would be minimal and just contain something like:

```
<!DOCTYPE html>
<html>
<head>
    <title>Yoursite</title>
    <script type="text/javascript">
        var date = new Date();
        var offset = -date.getTimezoneOffset() / 60;
        var timeZone = 'UTC';
        if (offset < 0) {
            timeZone = "UTC" + offset;
        } else {
            timeZone = 'UTC+' + offset;
        }
        document.cookie = 'userTimeZone=' + timeZone;
        window.location = '/home/?userTimeZone=' + timeZone;
    </script>
</head>
<body>
    <a href="@Url.Action("Front")">Visit main page</a>
</body>
</html>
```

This page allows us to do the following:

- Detect if cookies are supported (no cookie is set in the server, but the query string parameter is present)
- Detect if scripts are supported (neither query string or cookie is present)
- Gracefully fallback (clicked on the link)

You can in other words use that to determine what to do, such as saying "Hello, stone age user. Get a new browser."

The following code is for ASP.NET MVC. If you want to try it out, create a new ASP.NET MVC project and change the included HomeController to the following. So at server side we can code something like:

```
public class HomeController : Controller
{
    public ActionResult Index(string userTimeZone)
    {
        var cookieTimeZone = Request.Cookies["userTimeZone"];
```

```
            var cookieValue = cookieTimeZone == null ? null :
cookieTimeZone.Value;
        if (cookieValue != userTimeZone && userTimeZone != null)
        {
            // Cookies are not supported.
        }

        if (userTimeZone == null)
        {
            // No support for scripts.
        }

        // now display the real page.
        return RedirectToAction("Front");
    }

    public ActionResult Front()
    {
        var cookieTimeZone = Request.Cookies["userTimeZone"];

        // default time zone
        var cookieValue = cookieTimeZone == null ? "UTC" :
cookieTimeZone.Value;
        ViewBag.Message = "Hello. You time zone is: " + cookieValue;
        return View();
    }

    public ActionResult About()
    {
        return View();
    }

}
```

We've now ensured that we get the user time zone in each HTTP request (thanks to the cookie). However, we have nothing in our web application that will load the time zone setting. Using the cookie everywhere would be not very DRY and would also couple our logic with the HTTP implementation.

Let's instead use a feature in ASP.NET MVC called Action Filter. Action filters allow you to apply logic to a set of requests (ranging from all requests to a specific action). We'll use the action filter to transfer the time zone from the cookie into something that we can use in the rest of our code.

To try it out, put the following code into a new class file at the root folder for simplicity.

```
public class TimeZoneFilterAttribute : ActionFilterAttribute
{
    public static void ReadCookie(HttpCookieCollection cookies)
```

```
        {
            var timeZoneCookie = cookies["userTimeZone"];

            if (timeZoneCookie == null
                || string.IsNullOrEmpty(timeZoneCookie.Value))
                return;

            UserTimeZone.SetTimeZone(timeZoneCookie.Value);
        }
        public override void OnActionExecuting(ActionExecutingContext
    filterContext)
        {
            var timeZoneCookie = filterContext.HttpContext
                                         .Request.Cookies["userTimeZone"];

            if (timeZoneCookie == null
                || string.IsNullOrEmpty(timeZoneCookie.Value))
                return;

            UserTimeZone.SetTimeZone(timeZoneCookie.Value);
        }


    }
```

To activate the filter we need to add it to **global.asax**:

```
public class MvcApplication : System.Web.HttpApplication
{
    public static void RegisterGlobalFilters(GlobalFilterCollection filters)
    {
        filters.Add(new HandleErrorAttribute());
        filters.Add(new TimeZoneFilterAttribute());

    }

}
```

In our filter we used another class called **UserTimeZone**, which is shown below. It's the class that we'll use each time we need to convert UTC to the user time zone. The class itself looks something like this:

```
public static class UserTimeZone
{
    [ThreadStatic]
    private static TimeZoneInfo _current;
```

```csharp
static UserTimeZone()
{
    DefaultTimeZone = TimeZoneInfo.Utc;
}

public static TimeZoneInfo DefaultTimeZone { get; set; }

public static TimeZoneInfo Instance
{
    get { return _current ?? DefaultTimeZone; }
    private set { _current = value; }
}

public static void SetTimeZone(string timeZone)
{
    // it's up to you to decide how invalid cookies should be handled.
    int hours;
    if (!int.TryParse(timeZone.Substring(4), out hours))
        return;

    var myOffset = TimeSpan.FromHours(hours);
    Instance = (from x in TimeZoneInfo.GetSystemTimeZones()
                where x.BaseUtcOffset == myOffset
                select x).First();

}

public static DateTime ToUserTime(this DateTime dateTime)
{
    return dateTime.Add(Instance.BaseUtcOffset);
}

public static DateTime FromUserTime(this DateTime dateTime)
{
    return dateTime.Subtract(Instance.BaseUtcOffset);
}

}
```

The **DefaultTimeZone** can be used to configure which time zone to use if none has been specified in the cookie. **ToUserTime()** converts a date/time from UTC to the user time zone while **FromUserTime()** converts the user-specified time to UTC.

The cool thing is that the filter will automatically configure that class for us. Hence we only need to use something like this:

```csharp
public ActionResult Front()
{
    var christmasNoonUtc = new DateTime(2012, 12, 14, 12, 00, 00);
```

```
    var msg = "Hello. When it's christmas noon at UTC, it's {0} at your
place.";
    ViewBag.Message = string.Format(msg, christmasNoonUtc.ToUserTime());

    return View();

}
```

Time zone through login

There is an alternative solution, which is a lot less complex: use a user login and let the user
configure the time zone in the settings. ASP.NET MVC and other libraries have login solutions
included in the project templates that are created.

You can just create a new option in the Settings page where users can choose their own time
zone.

You can still use the **UserTimeZone** class and an action filter from the previous section.

Date/time in form posts

Users might also specify date and time values in your HTML forms. Hence we need to convert
those dates from the user time zone to UTC. Wouldn't it be nice if that conversion was done
automatically?

That's possible, thanks to another feature in ASP.NET MVC. You can use the Model Binders
feature to convert HTML forms into your view models or action arguments.

So what we basically will do is to override the default model binder for date/time and
automatically convert the dates to UTC. It looks like this:

```
public class DateTimeModelBinder : DefaultModelBinder
{
    public override object BindModel(ControllerContext controllerContext,
                                     ModelBindingContext bindingContext)
    {
        var value = base.BindModel(controllerContext, bindingContext);
        if (value is DateTime)
        {
            return ((DateTime)value).FromUserTime();
        }

        return value;
    }
}
```

To active it, we have to tell MVC to use that binder for date/time. The configuration is usually made in **global.asax**.

```
protected void Application_Start()
{
    AreaRegistration.RegisterAllAreas();

    RegisterGlobalFilters(GlobalFilters.Filters);
    RegisterRoutes(RouteTable.Routes);

    ModelBinders.Binders.Add(typeof(DateTime), new DateTimeModelBinder());

}
```

Done. Every time we get a date/time now, we'll get it as UTC (as long as the action filter has done its job).

One problem though: the action filters are executed after model binders. Hence the user time zone has not been set when the binder is running. So the time zone will not been specified. I've not come up with a better solution than to invoke the filter and supply the cookie from the binder.

And that's to use a custom HTTP module. Since ASP.NET 4 (and the introduction of WebPages), there is a new way to automatically register HTTP modules, using a special attribute shown below.

```
[assembly:PreApplicationStartMethod(typeof(TimeZoneCookieWithFilter.TimeZoneH
ttpModule), "RegisterModule")]
namespace TimeZoneCookieWithFilter
{
    public class TimeZoneHttpModule : IHttpModule
    {
        public void Init(HttpApplication context)
        {
            context.BeginRequest += OnRequest;
        }

        public static void RegisterModule()
        {
            DynamicModuleUtility.RegisterModule(typeof(TimeZoneHttpModule));
        }

        public static void ReadCookie(HttpCookieCollection cookies)
        {
            var timeZoneCookie = cookies["userTimeZone"];

            if (timeZoneCookie == null
                || string.IsNullOrEmpty(timeZoneCookie.Value))
                return;
```

```
            UserTimeZone.SetTimeZone(timeZoneCookie.Value);
        }

        private void OnRequest(object sender, EventArgs e)
        {
            var app = (HttpApplication) sender;
            var timeZoneCookie = app.Request.Cookies["userTimeZone"];

            if (timeZoneCookie == null
                || string.IsNullOrEmpty(timeZoneCookie.Value))
                return;

            UserTimeZone.SetTimeZone(timeZoneCookie.Value);
        }

        public void Dispose()
        {

        }
    }
}
```

That will automatically initialize the user time zone before the model binders. All user-submitted dates will now be in UTC when your action methods are invoked.

If you are using a framework that has View Models, use them to convert the dates to the user time zone before displaying.

Chapter 5 Numbers

As first glance, numbers might seem to be the same for different cultures. But they do differ when it comes to separators and grouping.

One million comma fifty is in Swedish "1 000 000,50" while it's "1,000,000.50" in the United States.

.NET

Among the others, in .NET we use the **ToString()** method to do the formatting. I recommend that you try to use the built-in formatters instead of manually defining the grouping etc.

Let's print a million and a half:

```
var se = new CultureInfo("sv-SE");
var us = new CultureInfo("en-US");
var number = 1000000.5;

Console.WriteLine("SE: {0}", number.ToString("N", se));
Console.WriteLine("US: {0}", number.ToString("N", us));
```

The result follows:

Figure 32: Number output

You could have done the same example by specifying the grouping manually:

```
var se = new CultureInfo("sv-se");
var us = new CultureInfo("en-us");
var number = 1000000.5;

Console.WriteLine("SE: {0}", number.ToString(@"#,#.0", se));
Console.WriteLine("US: {0}", number.ToString(@"#,#.0", us));
```

This results in:

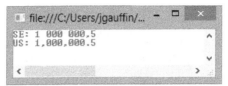

Figure 33: Numbers formatting

The comma tells .NET to use digit grouping, and the ".0" is used to tell how many decimals to use. You can read more about number formatting in MSDN.

JavaScript

At first, formatting numbers in JavaScript seems to be easy. There is a function called **toLocaleString(culture)**, which should work just fine. Unfortunately, the support is not great in all browsers. And it also depends on which languages the user has activated in the web browser.

Let's take a simple example. Add the following code into an empty HTML page.

```
<script type="text/javascript">
    var number = 1000000.50;
    document.writeln(number.toLocaleString('sv-SE') + "<br>");
    document.writeln(number.toLocaleString('en-US') + "<br>");
</script>
```

The output from that script looks quite nice in Google Chrome, as shown in Figure 34:

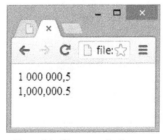

Figure 34: Chrome output

But the output in IE is a bit lacking (but IE get a bonus point for the decimal formatting), as shown in Figure 35:

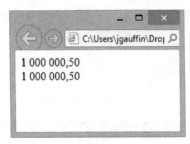

Figure 35: Internet Explorer output

The Swedish formatting is used for the U.S. culture, too. The reason is that IE ignores the culture argument and uses the culture that is configured in Windows.

Globalize

Since we have Globalize, we can get a bit more straightforward conversion.

```
<!DOCTYPE html>
<html xmlns="http://www.w3.org/1999/xhtml">
<head>
    <title></title>
    <script src="Scripts/jquery-1.9.1.min.js"></script>
    <script src="Scripts/jquery.globalize/globalize.js"></script>
    <script src="Scripts/jquery.globalize/cultures/globalize.culture.se-
SE.js"></script>
</head>
<body>
    <script type="text/javascript">
        Globalize.culture("se-SE");
        document.writeln(Globalize.format(1000000.1, "n") + "<br>");
        Globalize.culture("en-US");
        document.write(Globalize.format(1000000.1, "n"));
    </script>
</body>
</html>
```

The result follows:

Figure 36: Globalize output

Chapter 6 Currency/Money

There is no built-in support for currencies in .NET. The recommended approach is to use the **decimal** data type. That can however be a pain if you have to support multiple currencies.

```csharp
static void Main(string[] args)
{
    decimal shoppingCartTotal = 100;

    var us = new CultureInfo("en-US");
    Console.WriteLine("Is it {0} ..", shoppingCartTotal.ToString("C0", us));

    var sv = new CultureInfo("sv-SE");
    Console.WriteLine(".. or {0}", shoppingCartTotal.ToString("C0", sv));

}
```

The result is shown in Figure 37:

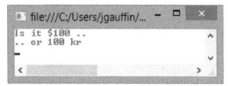

Figure 37: Currency formatting

The "0" in "C0" is for no decimals.

Handling multiple currencies

If you have to manage multiple currencies, always make sure that you include the currency identifier in all classes that contain amounts. Otherwise it's easy to use the incorrect currency (which might be worth less).

A better approach would be to create a **Money** struct that can be used instead. The struct can be found in the Appendix.

```csharp
class Program
{
    static void Main(string[] args)
    {
        var amountSek = new Money(500, "sv-se");
```

```
        var amountUsd = new Money(500, "en-us");

        Console.WriteLine("Is '{0}' equal '{1}'? {2}", amountSek, amountUsd,
amountSek.Equals(amountUsd));


        amountSek += 500;
        Console.WriteLine("New amount: " + amountSek);

        Console.ReadLine();
    }

}
```

The result follows:

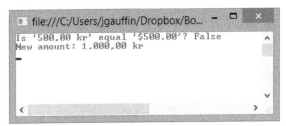

Figure 38: Using the money struct

JavaScript

It might surprise you that JavaScript itself has quite good support for currency. Some initial attempts might look like this:

```
<script type="text/javascript">
    var amount = 5.382;
    document.writeln("Total amount: " + amount.toFixed(2));

</script>
```

We get the following result:

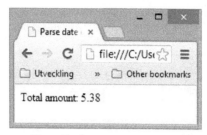

Figure 39: Javascript money

However, there is a much more elegant way:

```
<script type="text/javascript">
    var amount = 5.382;
    document.writeln("Total amount: " + amount.toLocaleString('sv-se', {
style: 'currency' }));
</script>
```

This will produce the following output:

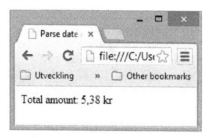

Figure 40: Formatted money

Notice that the decimal separator is correct for my language, and that the correct currency is attached.

Also notice that again, IE uses the OS (Windows) culture.

Chapter 7 Text

Text. Is that really something that we have to discuss? Isn't it all about saving texts in different languages? Unfortunately, no.

String comparisons

Let's start with a simple exercise. What will the resulting variable contain – true or false?

```
class Program
{
    static void Main(string[] args)
    {
        var result = "i".Equals("I",
StringComparison.CurrentCultureIgnoreCase);
        Console.WriteLine("Result is: " + result);
    }

}
```

It will return false if you live in Turkey. You could have done the comparison like this:

```
class Program
{
    static void Main(string[] args)
    {
        var result = "i".Equals("I", StringComparison.OrdinalIgnoreCase);
        Console.WriteLine("Result is: " + result);
    }

}
```

This will return true for all countries.

Know your target audience or what you want to get out of string comparisons. Letters that might seem obvious to you might work differently for someone else.

Different types of letters and alphabets

U.S. citizens have been spared from Latin characters, but most of the European countries have not. And to make it more complex, many European countries uses different sets of Latin characters.

In Sweden we use "åäö" while in France they use "àâæçéèêëïîôœùûüÿ". And that's just two of the countries in Europe. Then we have the rest of the world, with several different alphabets.

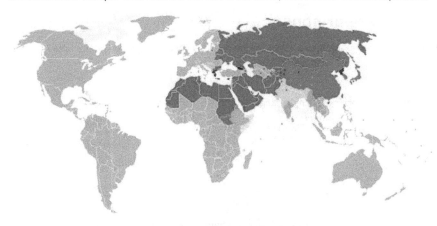

(Image from _Wikipedia_).

Alphabets: Armenian , Cyrillic , Georgian , Greek , Latin , Latin (and Arabic) , Latin and Cyrillic
Abjads: Arabic , Hebrew
Abugidas: North Indic , South Indic , Ge'ez , Tāna , Canadian Syllabic and Latin
Logographic+syllabic: Pure logographic , Mixed logographic and syllabaries , Featural-alphabetic syllabary + limited logographic , Featural-alphabetic syllabary

Encodings

In the beginning there was ASCII (American Standard Code for International Interchange), which was a 7-bit text encoding. It couldn't represent accent characters such as 'ä'. Here is a Swedish sentence:

—Hej alla barn, jag heter Rulle! Jag är full – full Rulle! Hej då!

To solve the problem with accents, another method of encoding called Extended ASCII (or 8bit ASCII) was introduced. It was later replaced with iso-8559-1 (ISO Latin 1), which worked for most western European countries. These encodings are still simple, since only one byte is used per character.

Those encodings are not enough, since many countries have extended character sets.

你好世界

That text says "hello world" in Chinese (I hope; these Chinese characters were generated using Google Translate).

If you want to know the 99.5 percent most frequently used Chinese characters, you have to learn 3,500 different ones. As you might have figured out, all of those characters won't fit into a single byte.

Unicode

A new standard has emerged to solve this problem, a version of Unicode called UTF8. UTF8 was designed to be compatible with ASCII. That is, the most frequently used ASCII characters are encoded in the same way in UTF8. The great thing with that is that many text parsers (like an HTML parser) don't have to know about the encoding, as those bytes look the same as in ASCII (i.e. <html> looks the same in both ASCII and UTF8).

UTF8 has also become the default encoding in many programming languages (and in HTML).

Unicode comes in different flavors. The name of each version reflects how many bytes it requires. UTF8 requires one byte (8 bits = 1 byte). UTF16 gets a minimum of two bytes per character, and UTF32 requires four bytes. Which one to use depends on the alphabet that you want to support.

.NET

In .NET we have the **System.Text** namespace where all different encodings are located. In that namespace there is a class that contains a couple of static properties to make our life easier.

.NET itself uses UTF16 as internal encoding for the **String** class. Do note that **System.IO.StreamWriter** and other classes use UTF8 per default.

Let's prove what I said about the encodings by printing the bytes that they generate:

```
class Program
{
    static void Main(string[] args)
    {
        var text = "Hello world";
        var utf8 = Encoding.UTF8.GetBytes(text);
```

```
        var ascii = Encoding.ASCII.GetBytes(text);
        var utf16 = Encoding.Unicode.GetBytes(text);
        var utf32 = Encoding.UTF32.GetBytes(text);

        Console.WriteLine("UTF8:   " + string.Join(",", utf8));
        Console.WriteLine();
        Console.WriteLine("ASCII: " + string.Join(",", ascii));
        Console.WriteLine();
        Console.WriteLine("UTF16:  " + string.Join(",", utf16));
        Console.WriteLine();
        Console.WriteLine("UTF32:  " + string.Join(",", utf32));

    }
}
```

As you can see in Figure 41, UTF8 and ASCII are identical while UTF16/32 takes up more space:

```
file:///C:/Users/jgauffin/Documents/Visual Studio 2012/Projects/ConsoleApplica...  -  □  ×
UTF8:   72,101,108,108,111,32,119,111,114,108,100
ASCII: 72,101,108,108,111,32,119,111,114,108,100
UTF16:  72,0,101,0,108,0,108,0,111,0,32,0,119,0,111,0,114,0,108,0,100,0
UTF32:  72,0,0,0,101,0,0,0,108,0,0,0,108,0,0,0,111,0,0,0,32,0,0,0,119,0,0,0,111,0
,0,0,114,0,0,0,108,0,0,0,100,0,0,0
```

Figure 41: Encoding output

Resource files

Resource files are special files that contain different types of resources like images and text. These files can be used for localization when you create multiple copies of them. Each copy of the file represents a specific culture.

To add a resource file, right-click on the project in the Solution Explorer, click **Add**, and then click **New item**. Next, find **Resource file** in the list and give it a name like shown below

Figure 42: New resource file

The file itself contains something called a string table. It's a mapping between identifiers and the strings that they represent. The identifier itself must remain the same for all different resource rules. An example follows:

Figure 43: Add a string to the resource file

You can finally use the string:

```csharp
class Program
{
    static void Main(string[] args)
    {
        Console.WriteLine(MyStrings.Hello);

        Console.ReadLine();
    }
}
```

Visual Studio automatically generates the **MyStrings** class and names it as the resource file. The class contains all resources in the resource file and acts as an accessor. VB.NET has a custom class named **My** that is used to access resources. More information about this class is available in MSDN.

The resources themselves are accessed from a special class called a **ResourceManager**. You can access that file using **MyStrings.RecourceManager**. I'll come back to that later.

That above code example was for one language only. To add support for multiple languages, you just copy the language file and give it a new name with a language code suffix. The file without a prefix is used as the default language file, as illustrated in Figure 44.

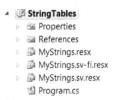

Figure 44: Resource file naming

Notice that I created one file with the "sv" suffix and one with the "sv-FI" suffix. That means that anyone speaking Swedish in Finland will get their own language while users from all other Swedish-speaking countries get a neutral dialect (the "sv" file). Everyone else can use the file without a language suffix.

How do you specify the language to use? You do it using the **CultureInfo** class, as described previously.

```csharp
class Program
{
    static void Main(string[] args)
    {
        Thread.CurrentThread.CurrentUICulture = new CultureInfo("sv-FI");
        Console.WriteLine(MyStrings.Hello);

        Thread.CurrentThread.CurrentUICulture = new CultureInfo("sv");
        Console.WriteLine(MyStrings.Hello);

        Thread.CurrentThread.CurrentUICulture = new CultureInfo("en-US");
        Console.WriteLine(MyStrings.Hello);

        Console.ReadLine();
    }
}
```

The output is:

Figure 45: String handling

The string outputted is the one that I've written in the respective resource file.

ASP.NET (WebForms)

In ASP.NET we also use string tables. They are divided into two different sections: local resources and global resources.

Global resources

Global resources can be shared between pages. You can use the static accessors just as with regular string tables (i.e. **MyResourceFile.MyTextName**).

However, the global resources are placed in a special file inside the ASP.NET projects. To add the folder, right-click on the project in the Solution Explorer, click **Add ASP.NET Folder**, and then click **Add**, as shown in the following figure:

Figure 46: Add new resource

That adds the global resources folder to which you can add global resource files, as shown in Figure 47.

Figure 47: Added file

The following example illustrates a resource string usage:

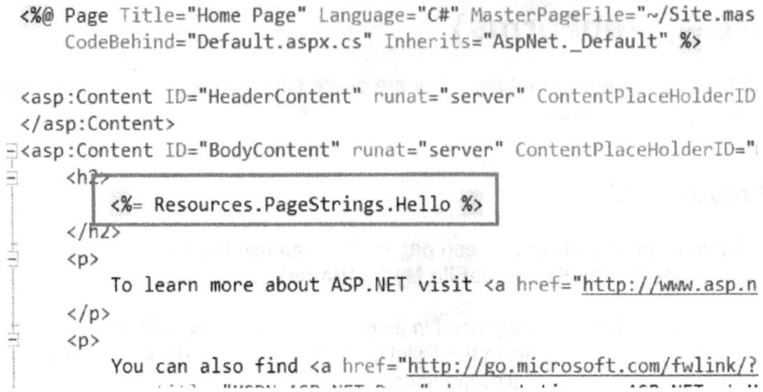

```
<%@ Page Title="Home Page" Language="C#" MasterPageFile="~/Site.mas
    CodeBehind="Default.aspx.cs" Inherits="AspNet._Default" %>

<asp:Content ID="HeaderContent" runat="server" ContentPlaceHolderID
</asp:Content>
<asp:Content ID="BodyContent" runat="server" ContentPlaceHolderID="
    <h2>
        <%= Resources.PageStrings.Hello %>
    </h2>
    <p>
        To learn more about ASP.NET visit <a href="http://www.asp.n
    </p>
    <p>
        You can also find <a href="http://go.microsoft.com/fwlink/?
```

Figure 48: Resource usage example

Local resources

Local resources are resources that are specific for each page. They cannot be shared between several pages. The cool thing with local resources is that you can use them in a convention over configuration manner.

First, create a simple page (I used the default WebForms template in VS2012):

```
<%@ Page Title="" Language="C#" MasterPageFile="~/Site.Master"
AutoEventWireup="true" CodeBehind="DemoForm.aspx.cs"
Inherits="WebApplication2.DemoForm1" %>

<asp:Content ID="Content1" ContentPlaceHolderID="HeadContent" runat="server">
</asp:Content>
<asp:Content ID="Content2" ContentPlaceHolderID="FeaturedContent"
runat="server">
</asp:Content>
<asp:Content ID="Content3" ContentPlaceHolderID="MainContent" runat="server">

    <!-- Note the meta:resourcekey -->
    <asp:Button ID="SomeButton" runat="server" Text="Not localized"
meta:resourcekey="SomeButton" />

</asp:Content>
```

The meta resource key is the string that tells us what to find. ASP.NET will look for that key in a resource file, which got the exact name as the ASPX file, as shown in Figure 49.

Figure 49: Page resources

In that file you should add every property of every control that you want localized. I've just added the Text property of the button in the following example:

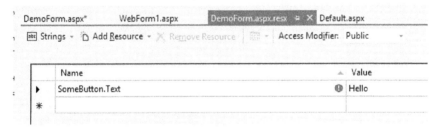

Figure 50: Button text

The result is shown in Figure 51:

Figure 51: Output

Read more in <u>MSDN</u> or in <u>MSDN Magazine</u>. The MSDN Magazine article targets .NET 2.0, but is still valid.

Auto selecting culture

You can get ASP.NET to automatically select a culture for you by using the ones provided by your web browser.

In Google Chrome I've configured my languages as follows:

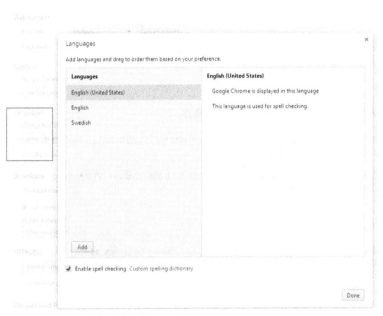

Figure 52: Chrome settings

These settings are included in the web request like this:

Figure 53: Accept-language header

To get ASP.NET to use those values, we have to open up web.config and find globalization under system.Web.

```
<configuration>
  <system.web>
    <globalization culture="auto" uiCulture="auto" />

    <compilation debug="true" targetFramework="4.5" />
    <httpRuntime targetFramework="4.5" />
  </system.web>
</configuration>
```

ASP.NET MVC & WebApi

ASP.NET and WebApi use similar techniques for localization, so I will document their approaches in the same section.

There are three different sections that can be translated in MVC/WebApi. Each section uses its own solution for the localization.

Views

The recommended approach for views is to use string tables as for regular ASP.NET projects. Create a file under global resources and access it using the generated static class as shown in the following figure.

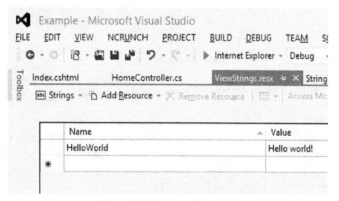

Figure 54: New resource

Next, create a new view in which you use that resource file:

```
@using Resources
@{
    ViewBag.Title = "Index";
}

<h2>Index</h2>

<p>@ViewStrings.HelloWorld</p>
```

Running the application would display the following text:

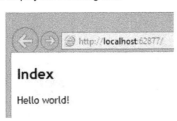

Figure 55: Resource string output

View models

View models in ASP.NET MVC can also be localized. The strings are still stored in resource files. But as there is no way to globally specify a resource file (or even per view model), you have to repeat the specification for each model.

Start by creating a new resource file and specifying the strings.

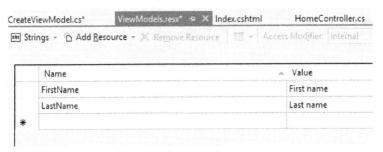

Figure 56: Resource strings

Next, create a new view model:

```
namespace MvcModels.Models.Users
{
    public class CreateViewModel
```

```
    {
        public string FirstName { get; set; }
        public string LastName { get; set; }
    }

}
```

To create a connection between the view model and the string table, we use an attribute called [Display]. In it we specify which resource file to use and what the field is called:

```
namespace MvcModels.Models.Users
{
    public class CreateViewModel
    {
        [Display(ResourceType = typeof(Resources.ViewModels), Name =
"FirstName")]
        public string FirstName { get; set; }

        [Display(ResourceType = typeof(Resources.ViewModels), Name =
"LastName")]
        public string LastName { get; set; }
    }

}
```

There is however one problem. Resource files are by default compiled as internal classes. That doesn't work well with the attributes, since they exist in the **System.ComponentModel.DataAnnotations** assembly. Hence we need to reconfigure the resource file to generate a public class.

Right-click on the resource file in the Solution Explorer and select **Properties**. Change the settings so that the **Custom Tool** is set to **PublicResXFileCodeGenerator** and the **Custom Tool Namespace** is set to **Resources**. Finally, change the **Build Action** to **Embedded Resource**. The project should now be able to run.

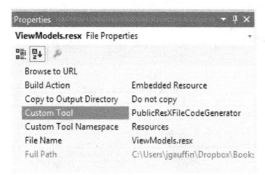

Figure 57: Resource file changes

Validation messages

Validation messages work in a similar fashion. We use string tables and attributes to specify that the validation messages should use resource files to get the localized strings.

If we build on the previous example we get the following view model:

```
namespace MvcValidation.Models.Users
{
    public class CreateViewModel
    {
        [Display(ResourceType = typeof(Resources.ViewModels), Name =
"FirstName")]
        [Required(ErrorMessageResourceType = typeof(Resources.ViewModels),
ErrorMessageResourceName = "Required")]
        public string FirstName { get; set; }

        [Display(ResourceType = typeof(Resources.ViewModels), Name =
"LastName")]
        [Required(ErrorMessageResourceType = typeof(Resources.ViewModels),
ErrorMessageResourceName = "Required")]
        [StringLength(20, ErrorMessageResourceType =
typeof(Resources.ViewModels), ErrorMessageResourceName = "StringLength")]
        public string LastName { get; set; }
    }
}
```

The string table looks like this:

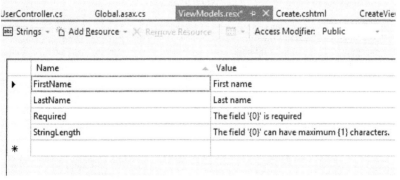

Figure 58: String table

If you look closely, you will see that we are now using formatters (the "{0}" strings). The number of arguments depends on the number of arguments used in the validation attribute constructor. The first argument will always be the property name, while the other arguments depend on the constructor.

The end result is:

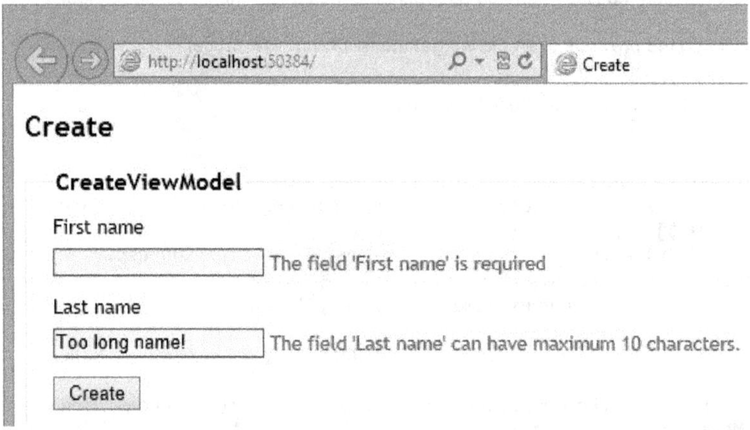

Figure 59: Validation messages

Alternatives to string tables

If you would like to use an alternative to string tables you either need to stop using Data Annotations (since there really is no way to extend its localization handling) or start using a third-party library (which needs to use some sort of hack). There is no other way.

As for the first option, I recommend that you look at the Fluent Validation library, which can be found on CodePlex at: http://fluentvalidation.codeplex.com/.

For the latter, I've created a library called *Griffin.MvcContrib* that can be used to use any data source for the strings. With it you do not have to specify the resource files but can revert to just using validation attributes. Do note that I use some hacks in it to allow you to keep using the validation attributes as Microsoft intended.

Your models look clean:

```
namespace GriffinMvcContrib.Models.User
{
    public class CreateViewModel
    {
        [Required]
        public string FirstName { get; set; }
```

```
        [Required]
        [StringLength(10)]
        public string LastName { get; set; }
    }

}
```

You can read about the library in gihub if you are interested in learning more.

Switching languages

Sometimes you do not want to use the culture specified by the browser (as shown in the "Auto selecting culture" example).

You can create a nifty little HTTP module, which allows you to switch languages by using the query string. Simply add a new value called "lang" like shown in the following figure:

Figure 60: Switch language using the URL

That string will be picked up by the module and stored in a cookie. The actual handling is therefore transparent to your application.

The HTTP module is automatically loaded into ASP.NET and will automatically set the correct cultures for you.

The module:

```
using System;
using System.Globalization;
using System.Threading;
using System.Web;
using Microsoft.Web.Infrastructure.DynamicModuleHelper;

[assembly:
PreApplicationStartMethod(typeof(ExampleApp.LanguageSwitcherModule),
"Setup")]

namespace ExampleApp
{
    public class LanguageSwitcherModule : IHttpModule
    {
```

```csharp
        private const string CookieName = "LangCookie";

        public static void Setup()
        {
DynamicModuleUtility.RegisterModule(typeof(LanguageSwitcherModule));
        }

        public void Init(HttpApplication context)
        {
            context.BeginRequest += OnRequest;
        }

        public void Dispose()
        {
        }

        private void OnRequest(object sender, EventArgs e)
        {
            var app = (HttpApplication) sender;

            // language switched
            if (app.Request.QueryString["lang"] != null)
            {
                var lang = app.Request.QueryString["lang"];
                AssignLanguage(lang);
                SetCookie(app.Response, lang);
            }

            // same language as before.
            else if (app.Request.Cookies[CookieName] != null)
            {
                AssignLanguage(app.Request.Cookies[CookieName].Value);
            }
        }

        private static void AssignLanguage(string lang)
        {
            Thread.CurrentThread.CurrentCulture =
                Thread.CurrentThread.CurrentUICulture =
                    new CultureInfo(lang);
        }

        private static void SetCookie(HttpResponse response, string language)
        {
            response.Cookies.Add(new HttpCookie(CookieName, language)
                {
                    Expires = DateTime.Now.AddYears(1),
                });
        }
```

```
        }
    }
}
```

Web sites

When working with web sites you typically use the `lang` attribute on the HTML element to specify the language that the HTML document is in. You can also use that element in javascripts to specify which language to load.

```
<html lang="x-klingon">
<head>
    <title>tlhIngan maH!</title>
</head>
<body>
    <h1>nuqneH</h1>
    <p>nuqDaq 'oH puchpa''e'</p>
</body>
</html>
```

An x is actually a valid tag, and means that the language is experimental. So what the `lang` tag says is that we are use an experimental language with the dialect "Klingon."

Otherwise you use any of the tags defined in the HTML5 specification (HTML4 uses the same type of code).

JavaScript plugins

JavaScript plugins can be localized by using a global extension to your plugin.

You typically begin by creating a plugin (myplugin.js):

```
var MyPlugin = (function() {
    function checkName(name) {
        if (name === 'Jonas') {
            return 'Kungen';
        } else {
            return name;
        }
    }
    function MyPlugin()
    {
    }
```

```
        MyPlugin.prototype.print = function(name) {
                name = checkName(name);
                return  MyPlugin.Texts.Welcome.replace('{name}', name);
        }


        return MyPlugin;
})();

// Initialize default language.
if (!MyPlugin.Texts) {
        MyPlugin.Texts = {};
        MyPlugin.Texts.Welcome = 'Hello, {name} is in the house.';
}
```

Then you add one or more languages in separate files (myplugin.sv-se.js)

```
MyPlugin.Texts.Welcome = 'Hej, {name} har äntligen kommit.';
```

Finally, you can select the correct language file by using the same technique as before:

```
<html lang="sv-se">
<head>
        <title>Javascript example</title>
        <script src="plugin.js"></script>

    <!-- use your server side language to get the correct language code -->
        <script src="plugin.sv-se.js"></script>
</head>
<body>
        <script type="text/javascript">
                var plugin =  new MyPlugin();
                document.writeln(plugin.print('Jonas'));
        </script>
</body>

</html>
```

This approach makes it easy to localize scripts. Simply copy the default language or any other to a separate file. The one making the localization can just replace the new texts. It also allows your users (if you are a plugin developer) to localize your plugin without effort.

Appendix

The DateTime extension methods for time zones

```
/// <summary>
///     Extensions for working with time zones with the regular
<c>DateTime</c> class.
/// </summary>
public static class DateTimeExtension
{
    /// <summary>
    ///     Converts from the specified time zone to UTC
    /// </summary>
    /// <param name="instance">Date/time in the specified time zone</param>
    /// <param name="timezoneName">
    ///     Name of the timezone. Must be one of the names in the registry,
for instance <c>W. Europe Standard Time</c>
    /// </param>
    /// <returns>UTC time</returns>
    /// <remarks>
    ///     <para>
    ///         You can list all time zones by using
<c>TimeZoneInfo.GetSystemTimeZones()</c>.
    ///     </para>
    /// </remarks>
    public static DateTime ToUniveralTime(this DateTime instance, string
timezoneName)
    {
        var tz = TimeZoneInfo.FindSystemTimeZoneById(timezoneName);
        if (tz == null)
            throw new ArgumentOutOfRangeException("timezoneName",
timezoneName, "Time zone was not found.");

        return TimeZoneInfo.ConvertTimeToUtc(instance, tz);
    }

    /// <summary>
    ///     Converts from the specified time zone to UTC
    /// </summary>
    /// <param name="instance">Date/time in the specified time zone</param>
    /// <param name="baseOffset">The base offset, DST should not be used in
this offset.</param>
    /// <returns>
    ///     UTC time
    /// </returns>
    /// <exception cref="System.ArgumentOutOfRangeException">baseOffset;A
```

```csharp
time zone with that baseoffset was not found.</exception>
    /// <remarks>
    ///         You can list all time zones by using
<c>TimeZoneInfo.GetSystemTimeZones()</c>.
    /// </remarks>
    public static DateTime ToUniveralTime(this DateTime instance, TimeSpan
baseOffset)
    {
        var tz = TimeZoneInfo.GetSystemTimeZones().FirstOrDefault(x =>
x.BaseUtcOffset == baseOffset);
        if (tz == null)
            throw new ArgumentOutOfRangeException("baseOffset", baseOffset,
                                        "A time zone with that
baseoffset was not found.");

        return TimeZoneInfo.ConvertTimeToUtc(instance, tz);
    }


    /// <summary>
    ///         Converts UTC to the specified time zone
    /// </summary>
    /// <param name="instance">Date in UTC format</param>
    /// <param name="timezoneName">
    ///         Name of the timezone. Must be one of the names in the registry,
for instance <c>W. Europe Standard Time</c>
    /// </param>
    /// <returns>Local time</returns>
    /// <remarks>
    ///         <para>
    ///             You can list all time zones by using
<c>TimeZoneInfo.GetSystemTimeZones()</c>.
    ///         </para>
    /// </remarks>
    public static DateTime ToLocalTime(this DateTime instance, string
timezoneName)
    {
        var tz = TimeZoneInfo.FindSystemTimeZoneById(timezoneName);
        if (tz == null)
            throw new ArgumentOutOfRangeException("timezoneName",
timezoneName, "Time zone was not found.");

        return TimeZoneInfo.ConvertTimeFromUtc(instance, tz);
    }

    /// <summary>
    ///         Converts UTC to the specified time zone
    /// </summary>
    /// <param name="instance">Date in UTC format</param>
    /// <param name="baseOffset">The base offset, DST should not be used in
```

this offset.</param>
```
    /// <returns>
    ///     Local time
    /// </returns>
    /// <exception cref="System.ArgumentOutOfRangeException">baseOffset;A
time zone with that baseoffset was not found.</exception>
    /// <remarks>
    ///     You can list all time zones by using
<c>TimeZoneInfo.GetSystemTimeZones()</c>.
    /// </remarks>
    public static DateTime ToLocalTime(this DateTime instance, TimeSpan
baseOffset)
    {
        var tz = TimeZoneInfo.GetSystemTimeZones().FirstOrDefault(x =>
x.BaseUtcOffset == baseOffset);
        if (tz == null)
            throw new ArgumentOutOfRangeException("baseOffset", baseOffset,
                                    "A time zone with that
baseoffset was not found.");

        return TimeZoneInfo.ConvertTimeFromUtc(instance, tz);
    }


    /// <summary>
    ///     Converts a date to RFC33339
    /// </summary>
    /// <param name="instance">The local DateTime instance (must be for the
time zone specified).</param>
    /// <param name="timezoneName">
    ///     Name of the timezone. Must be one of the names in the registry,
for instance <c>W. Europe Standard Time</c>
    /// </param>
    /// <returns>
    ///     For instance <c>2013-05-14T19:30:43+02:00</c> for Central
European Time when DST is active.
    /// </returns>
    /// <exception
cref="System.ArgumentOutOfRangeException">timezoneName;Time zone was not
found.</exception>
    /// <remarks>
    ///     <para>
    ///         This method also honors daylight saving time (i.e. adjusts
the offset during the summer).
    ///     </para>
    ///     <para>
    ///         You can list all time zones by using
<c>TimeZoneInfo.GetSystemTimeZones()</c>.
    ///     </para>
    /// </remarks>
```

```csharp
    public static string ToRFC3339(this DateTime instance, string
timezoneName)
    {
        var tz = TimeZoneInfo.FindSystemTimeZoneById(timezoneName);
        if (tz == null)
            throw new ArgumentOutOfRangeException("timezoneName",
timezoneName, "Time zone was not found.");

        var difference = tz.GetUtcOffset(instance);
        if (difference.TotalHours < 0.1 && difference.TotalHours > -0.1)
            return instance.ToString("yyyy-MM-ddTHH:mm:ssZ");

        var sign = difference.TotalHours < 0 ? "-" : "+";
        return instance.ToString("yyyy-MM-ddTHH:mm:ss") + sign +
difference.ToString(@"hh\:mm");
    }

    /// <summary>
    ///     Converts a date to RFC33339
    /// </summary>
    /// <param name="instance">The local DateTime instance (must be for the
time zone specified).</param>
    /// <param name="baseOffset">The base offset, DST should not be used in
this offset.</param>
    /// <returns>
    ///     For instance <c>2013-05-14T19:30:43+02:00</c> for Central
European Time when DST is active.
    /// </returns>
    /// <exception cref="System.ArgumentOutOfRangeException">baseOffset;A
time zone with that baseoffset was not found.</exception>
    /// <remarks>
    ///     <para>
    ///         This method also honors daylight saving time (i.e. adjusts
the offset during the summer).
    ///     </para>
    ///     <para>
    ///         You can list all time zones by using
<c>TimeZoneInfo.GetSystemTimeZones()</c>.
    ///     </para>
    /// </remarks>
    public static string ToRFC3339(this DateTime instance, TimeSpan
baseOffset)
    {
        var tz = TimeZoneInfo.GetSystemTimeZones().FirstOrDefault(x =>
x.BaseUtcOffset == baseOffset);
        if (tz == null)
            throw new ArgumentOutOfRangeException("baseOffset", baseOffset,
                                    "A time zone with that
baseoffset was not found.");
```

```
        var difference = tz.GetUtcOffset(instance);
        if (difference.TotalHours < 0.1 && difference.TotalHours > -0.1)
            return instance.ToString("yyyy-MM-ddTHH:mm:ssZ");

        var sign = difference.TotalHours < 0 ? "-" : "+";
        return instance.ToString("yyyy-MM-ddTHH:mm:ss") + sign +
difference.ToString(@"hh\:mm");
    }

}
```

The money struct

```
using System.Globalization;
public struct Money : IEquatable<Money>, IComparable, IComparable<Money>,
ICloneable
{
    private readonly decimal _amount;
    private readonly CultureInfo _cultureInfo;
    private readonly RegionInfo _regionInfo;

    public Money(decimal amount, string cultureName) : this(amount, new
CultureInfo(cultureName))
    {
    }

    public Money(decimal amount, CultureInfo cultureInfo)
    {
        if (cultureInfo == null) throw new
ArgumentNullException("cultureInfo");
        _cultureInfo = cultureInfo;
        _regionInfo = new RegionInfo(cultureInfo.LCID);
        _amount = amount;
    }

    public string ISOCurrencySymbol
    {
        get { return _regionInfo.ISOCurrencySymbol; }
    }

    public decimal Amount
    {
        get { return _amount; }
    }

    public int DecimalDigits
    {
```

```csharp
        get { return _cultureInfo.NumberFormat.CurrencyDecimalDigits; }
    }

    object ICloneable.Clone()
    {
        return new Money(_amount, _cultureInfo);
    }

    public int CompareTo(object obj)
    {
        if (obj == null) throw new ArgumentNullException("obj");
        if (!(obj is Money))
            throw new ArgumentException(string.Format("Argument must be of
type Money, got '{0}'.", obj));

        var other = (Money)obj;
        return CompareTo(other);
    }

    public int CompareTo(Money other)
    {
        if (this < other)
            return -1;
        return this > other ? 1 : 0;
    }

    public bool Equals(Money other)
    {
        if (ReferenceEquals(other, null)) return false;
        return ((ISOCurrencySymbol == other.ISOCurrencySymbol) && (_amount ==
other._amount));
    }

    public static bool operator >(Money first, Money second)
    {
        AssertSameCurrency(first, second);
        return first._amount > second._amount;
    }

    public static bool operator >=(Money first, Money second)
    {
        AssertSameCurrency(first, second);
        return first._amount >= second._amount;
    }

    public static bool operator <=(Money first, Money second)
    {
        AssertSameCurrency(first, second);
        return first._amount <= second._amount;
    }
```

```csharp
public static bool operator <(Money first, Money second)
{
    AssertSameCurrency(first, second);
    return first._amount < second._amount;
}

public static Money operator +(Money first, Money second)
{
    AssertSameCurrency(first, second);
    return new Money(first.Amount + second.Amount, first._cultureInfo);
}
public static Money operator +(Money first, decimal second)
{
    return new Money(first.Amount + second, first._cultureInfo);
}

public static Money Add(Money first, Money second)
{
    return first + second;
}

public static Money operator -(Money first, Money second)
{
    AssertSameCurrency(first, second);
    return new Money(first.Amount - second.Amount, first._cultureInfo);
}

public static Money Subtract(Money first, Money second)
{
    return first - second;
}

public override bool Equals(object obj)
{
    return (obj is Money) && Equals((Money) obj);
}

public override int GetHashCode()
{
    return _amount.GetHashCode() ^ _cultureInfo.GetHashCode();
}

private static void AssertSameCurrency(Money first, Money second)
{
    if (first == null) throw new ArgumentNullException("first");
    if (second == null) throw new ArgumentNullException("second");
    if (first.ISOCurrencySymbol != second.ISOCurrencySymbol)
        throw new FormatException(string.Format("Currency: {0}, other
currency: {1}", first.ISOCurrencySymbol,
```

```csharp
                                       second.ISOCurrencySymbol));
    }

    public static bool operator ==(Money first, Money second)
    {
        if (ReferenceEquals(first, second)) return true;
        if (ReferenceEquals(first, null) || ReferenceEquals(second, null))
return false;
        return Equals(first, second);
    }

    public static bool operator !=(Money first, Money second)
    {
        if (first == null) throw new ArgumentNullException("first");
        if (second == null) throw new ArgumentNullException("second");
        return !first.Equals(second);
    }

    public static Money operator *(Money money, decimal value)
    {
        if (money == null) throw new ArgumentNullException("money");

        return new Money(money.Amount*value, money._cultureInfo);
    }

    public static Money Multiply(Money money, decimal value)
    {
        if (money == null) throw new ArgumentNullException("money");
        return money*value;
    }

    public static Money operator /(Money money, decimal value)
    {
        if (money == null) throw new ArgumentNullException("money");

        return new Money(money.Amount/value, money._cultureInfo);
    }

    public static Money Divide(Money first, decimal value)
    {
        if (first == null) throw new ArgumentNullException("first");
        return first/value;
    }

    public Money Clone()
    {
        return new Money(_amount, _cultureInfo);
    }
```

```
    public override string ToString()
    {
        return Amount.ToString("C", _cultureInfo);
    }


    public string ToString(string format)
    {
        return Amount.ToString(format, _cultureInfo);
    }

}
```

Notes for class library developers

Resource files are great, but there is really no way to extend the localization features that they provide. As a class library developer, you are responsible for allowing your users to extend your library. When you use string tables, you make it very hard to extend the language handling.

A good example illustrating the problem is the validation library built into the .NET Framework: Data Annotations. Anyone who has tried to get localized validation messages with Data Annotation has most likely given up in frustration, and used the recommended approach by duplicating the string table specification for the attributes:

```
[Required(ErrorMessageResourceName = "CollectionName_Required",
ErrorMessageResourceType = typeof(Resource1))]
```

A simple solution is creating a singleton, which acts as a façade for the language handling. Something like **LanguageProvider.GetString**. The downside is that you can't use the compiled static variables that the language files provide, but instead you gain flexibility.

Internally you can still use string tables, but you also give the user the freedom to use his or her own solution.

The façade (façade pattern) looks like this:

```
public class LanguageProvider
{
    private static List<ILanguageProvider> _providers = new
List<ILanguageProvider>();
    private static ILanguageProvider _default = new
StringTableProvider(InternalResources.ResourceManager);

    public static string GetString(string name)
    {
```

```
        var providers = _providers;
        foreach (var provider in providers)
        {
            var str = provider.GetString(name);
            if (str != null)
                return str;

        }

        return _default.GetString(name) ?? name;
    }

    public static void Register(ILanguageProvider provider)
    {
        var providers = new List<ILanguageProvider>(_providers) {provider};
        _providers = providers;
    }
}
```

The **Register** method is used by the user to provide custom data sources while the **GetString** method is used to handle the translation. Notice that the default provider is just used as a fallback so the user can customize the built-in strings too.

The strings themselves are provided using classes, implementing the following interface:

```
public interface ILanguageProvider
{
    string GetString(string name);
}
```

A string table implementation would look like this:

```
public class StringTableProvider : ILanguageProvider
{
    private readonly ResourceManager _resourceManager;

    public StringTableProvider(ResourceManager resourceManager)
    {
        _resourceManager = resourceManager;
    }

    public string GetString(string name)
    {
        return _resourceManager.GetString(name);
    }

}
```

Finally, you can use the provider like this:

```
static void Main(string[] args)
{
    Console.WriteLine(LanguageProvider.GetString("SomeName"));
}
```

Unlike when using string tables directly, we do not get a compiled static class we can use, but instead we gain the flexibility to allow our users to customize the strings. You win some and you lose some.

www.ingramcontent.com/pod-product-compliance
Lightning Source LLC
Chambersburg PA
CBHW071304050326
40690CB00011B/2525